I WISH YOU a MERRY CHRISTMAS

MADE FOR YOU BY...

IT'S THE CHRISTMAS SEASON!

AND WHAT BETTER WAY TO GET
IN THE FESTIVE MOOD
THAN TO READ YOUR VERY OWN BOOK

ABOUT YOU, ME, AND ALL THINGS CHRISTMAS!?

YOU SEE, THIS BOOK
WAS WRITTEN JUST FOR YOU.

SO SIT BACK, PUT YOUR FEET UP,
GRAB A MUG OF HOT CHOCOLATE
AND A BAG OF MARSHMALLOWS,
AND READ TO YOUR HEART'S DESIRE!

WHY HAVE A NORMAL

SNOWBALL FIGHT

WHEN YOU CAN FILL
THE SNOWBALLS WITH

?

THREE PHRASES THAT SUM UP CHRISTMAS ARE:

_____

_____

_____,

LONG LINES GUARANTEED FOR LAST-MINUTE SHOPPERS, AND

_____.

NO ONE ENJOYS MAKING

WITH ME DURING THE HOLIDAYS MORE THAN YOU DO.

WE WOULD PROBABLY GIVE

A BAG FULL OF

....

FOR CHRISTMAS, BECAUSE

....

OUR DREAM
CHRISTMAS TREE
WOULD BE

. . . .

FEET TALL!

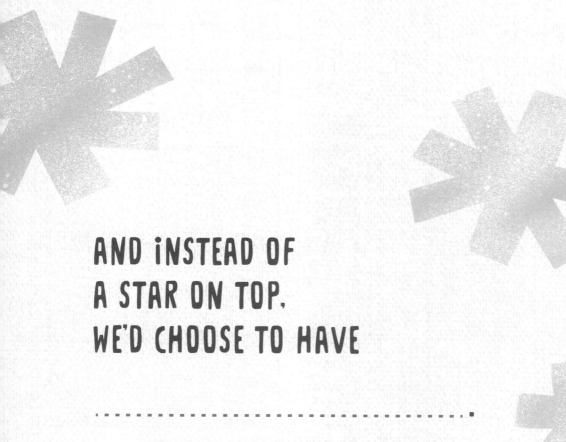

AND INSTEAD OF
A STAR ON TOP,
WE'D CHOOSE TO HAVE

....

ONE THING
I THINK
WE SHOULD DO
NEXT YEAR
AROUND THIS TIME,
THAT WE'VE NEVER DONE
BEFORE, IS

....

THE ONE THING
I ABSOLUTELY
DO NOT
WANT TO FIND
IN MY STOCKING IS

!

I LOVE MAKING

AROUND THIS
TIME OF YEAR!

IT'S NOT VERY HARD
TO MAKE, BUT IT'S
DELICIOUS!

HERE'S THE RECIPE :

ALL I WANT FOR
CHRISTMAS
IS MY TWO FRONT TEETH,
TWO HOURS OF

_____ TiME.

TWO BOTTLES OF

_____ ,

AND TWO GLASSES OF

_____ !

BUT WHAT I
ESPECIALLY WANT IS TWO

FILLED WITH

IF WE WERE
OUT TOGETHER AND SAW
A SNOW PiLE AS BiG AS A

-- ,

I'D MAKE SURE WE'D

------------------------------------- !

MY... **IDEA** OF GETTING INTO THE **CHRISTMAS SPIRIT** IS TO

IF WE WERE iN A
SNOWMAN
DECORATING CONTEST,
I'D BET WE'D WiN,
BECAUSE OUR SNOWMAN
WOULD HAVE

_____ AND _____.

AND WE MIGHT HAVE FORGOTTEN
TO BRING CARROTS, BUT WE'D USE A
_____ INSTEAD.

AND FOR HIS EYES, WE'D USE
_____ !

IF YOU WERE A RESIDENT OF
THE NORTH POLE,
YOU WOULD BE :
(CIRCLE ONE)

SANTA   AN ELF

MRS. CLAUS

A REINDEER

THE GINGERBREAD MAN

A PENGUIN   A POLAR BEAR

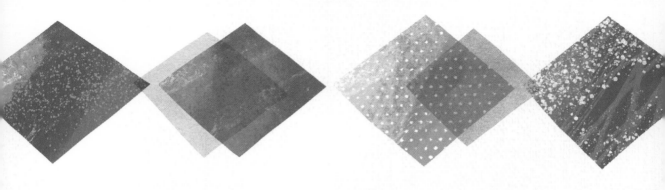

ONE YEAR, MY

WAS GIVEN A

FOR CHRISTMAS AND I WAS
SO JEALOUS!

THIS IS OUR **FAVORITE** THING TO DO IN THE SNOW TOGETHER!

I'VE ATTEMPTED TO DRAW THIS, SO **GOOD LUCK** FIGURING IT OUT!

IF THERE'S ONE THING YOU AND I HAVE LEARNED FOR SURE, IT'S THAT THIS

HOLIDAY

IS TOO DANG SHORT!

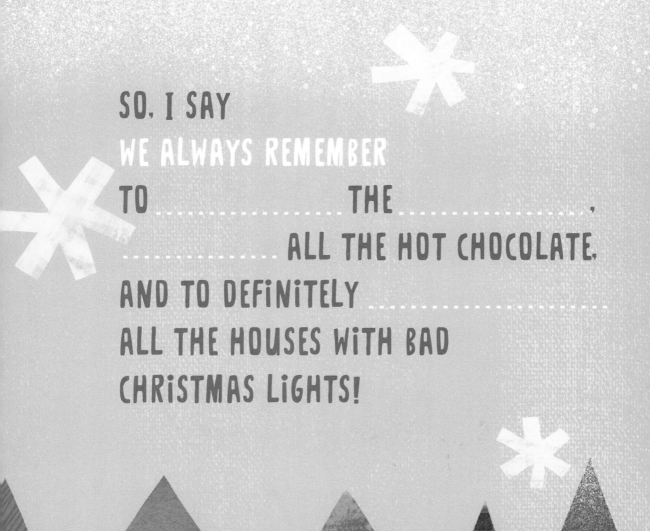

SO, I SAY
WE ALWAYS REMEMBER
TO .... THE .... ,
.... ALL THE HOT CHOCOLATE,
AND TO DEFINITELY ....
ALL THE HOUSES WITH BAD
CHRISTMAS LIGHTS!

CHRISTMAS
iS THE
TiME OF YEAR
WHEN KiDS

....

AND PARENTS

....

I THINK
WE SHOULD GIVE

..............................'S

NUMBER TO AN
ASSEMBLY FULL OF KIDS
AND TELL THEM IT'S
SANTA'S CELLPHONE.

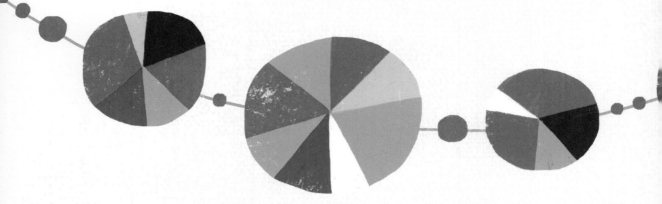

YOUR FAVORITE
REiNDEER
iS PROBABLY

,

BECAUSE

IF WE WERE A
CHRISTMAS TREAT, YOU WOULD BE

,

I WOULD BE

,

AND TOGETHER WE'D BE

.

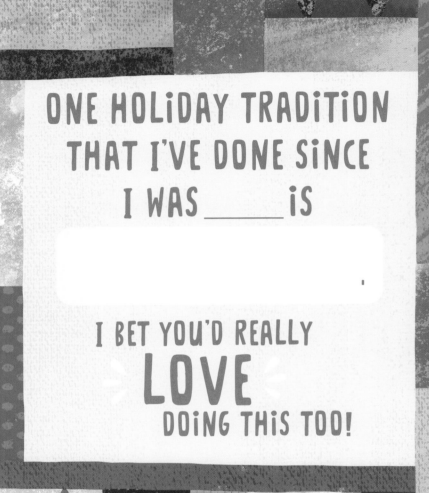

ONE HOLiDAY TRADITION
THAT I'VE DONE SINCE
I WAS _____ iS

I BET YOU'D REALLY
LOVE
DOING THiS TOO!

I WISH
YOU WOULD HAVE BEEN THERE
THIS ONE TIME I

ON CHRISTMAS MORNING!

THE BEST BOOK TO READ,
WHEN THE CHRISTMAS TREE
IS UP AND THE LIGHTS ARE ON
AND ALL IS
QUIET AND STILL, IS

BY

I KNOW
CHRISTMAS IS TECHNICALLY
ONLY ONE DAY,
BUT I REALLY THINK
IT SHOULD BE

DAYS LONG!

iS THE MOMENT
YOU STOP GETTING

_____

AND YOU START GETTING
A LOT MORE

_____ .

EVERYONE KNOWS ABOUT
DASHER, DANCER, PRANCER, VIXEN,
COMET, CUPID, DONNER, BLITZEN,
AND RUDOLPH!

BUT WHAT'S THE FUN IN THAT?
LET'S RENAME THEM ALL!

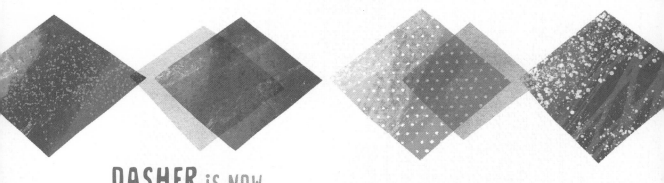

DASHER IS NOW ....,
DANCER IS ....,
PRANCER IS ....,
AND YOU'D PROBABLY
CHOOSE TO NAME **VIXEN**.............................
COMET WILL BE CALLED ....,
CUPID IS NOW ....,
DONNER WILL BE KNOWN AS ...., AND
BLITZEN IS NOW ....
YOU'D RENAME **RUDOLPH,** AND YOU'D PROBABLY CALL HIM
.............................!

THERE WAS THIS ONE
CHRISTMAS
WHERE EVERYTHING
SEEMED TO GO JUST
PERFECTLY.

IT ALL STARTED WHEN...

IF MY GIFT
TO YOU
COULD BE AN
HOUR-LONG LUNCH
WITH ANYONE
IN THE WORLD,
PAST OR PRESENT...

I'D MAKE SURE YOU HAD LUNCH WITH

_____,

AND I'D MAKE A RESERVATION
FOR THE TWO OF YOU AT

_____.

ONE CHRISTMAS EVENT
THAT I'VE NEVER GONE TO,
BUT HAVE ALWAYS WANTED TO,
is _____.

IT'S ALL
FUN AND GAMES
UNTIL
SANTA AND HIS ELVES

ALL I REALLY WANT FOR CHRISTMAS iS

.... ▪

AND I'M PRETTY SURE ALL YOU WANT FOR CHRISTMAS IS

....

JUST LIKE THE SNOWMAN CONTEST,
I THINK WE'D ALSO

WIN

THE GINGERBREAD HOUSE CONTEST.
'CAUSE OUR HOUSE
WOULD BE _____ FEET TALL,
THE WINDOWS WOULD BE MADE OF
_____,
AND THE FRONT DOOR OF_____.

THE ROOF WOULD HAVE

_____

ALL OVER IT, AND THE CHIMNEY
WOULD BE _____.
IT WOULD ALL WEIGH _____ POUNDS
WHEN WE WERE DONE WITH IT!

I REMEMBER THIS ONE
CHRISTMAS WHERE I SAW

- -

- iT WAS THE STRANGEST THING EVER!

YOU HAVE
TO KNOW
THIS STORY!

IF WE REWROTE THE
CLASSIC CHRISTMAS SONG
_____,

THE LYRICS WOULD READ
_____

AT THE BEGINNING
INSTEAD OF
_____.

IF I COULD PLAY

SANTA

JUST ONCE AND GIVE
A BAG OF COAL
TO ANYONE IN THE WORLD,
I'D GIVE IT TO

_____ .

ONE OF MY
FAVORITE
HOLIDAY MOVIES IS

....

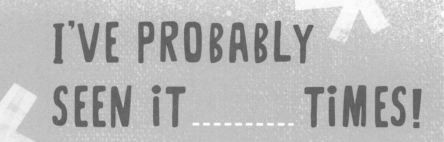

I'VE PROBABLY SEEN IT .... TIMES!

YOU HAVE TO WATCH IT!

'TIS THE SEASON
TO DRINK TOO MUCH

.... ,

LAUGH UNTIL YOU

....

EAT TOO MUCH

.... ,

AND TO BE EXTRA

....

I THINK THE REASON

SANTA

is ALWAYS SO DANG JOLLY

is REALLY BECAUSE

_____.

I KNOW _____

COSTS _____ DOLLARS, BUT

I'VE WANTED ONE FOR

CHRISTMAS

SINCE I WAS _____ YEARS OLD!

I STILL HAVEN'T GOTTEN ONE.

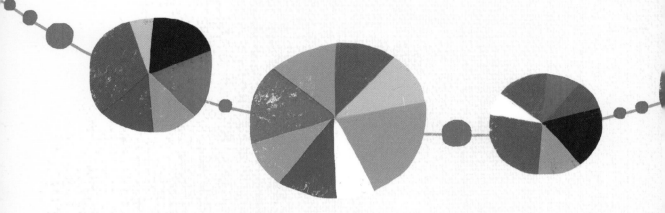

ONE OF
MY FAVORITE THINGS
THAT I EVER GAVE YOU FOR

CHRISTMAS

WAS ....

AND ONE OF
MY FAVORITE THINGS
THAT YOU EVER
GAVE ME WAS

....

THE CRAZIEST THING
I'VE EVER SEEN
SOMEONE DO AROUND
THIS TIME OF YEAR
WAS _____!

IF WE STOLE
SANTA'S
NAUGHTY LIST,
I DON'T THINK
WE WOULD BE
AT ALL SURPRISED
TO FIND _____'S
NAME IN THE #1 SPOT!

ONE CHRISTMAS DECORATION THAT I THINK IS VASTLY OVERRATED IS _____.

I SEE THEM EVERYWHERE NOW!

I'LL NEVER FORGET
WHEN WE _____
AT CHRISTMAS TIME!
THAT WAS SUCH A
_____ ¡DEA!

MY LETTER TO
SANTA
WOULD LOOK
SOMETHING
LIKE THIS:

DEAR SANTA,

I JUST WANTED TO LET YOU KNOW THAT I'VE BEEN
REALLY _____ THIS YEAR...
AND I _____ REGRET iT! I REALLY MADE SURE
TO _____ ALL THE _____ .
COULD YOU BLAME ME? ALSO, I KNOW YOU'RE SUPER
BUSY AND _____, BUT I JUST WANTED
TO REMiND YOU THAT A TALL BOTTLE OF _____
iS REALLY ALL I NEED. AND I COULD ALSO DO WiTH
SOME MAJOR _____. IS THIS TOO MUCH
TO ASK? IN PAYMENT, I'LL LEAVE YOU A FULL GLASS
OF MiLK AND COOKiES. AND BY MiLK, I MEAN _____ .
AND BY COOKiES, I MEAN _____, OF COURSE!

LOVE,

_____

AND IF I HAD TO GUESS, **SANTA'S LETTER** TO YOU THIS YEAR WOULD LOOK SOMETHING LIKE THIS:

DEAR _____,

I JUST WANTED TO LET YOU KNOW THAT
YOU'VE BEEN REALLY _____ THIS YEAR.
AFTER CHECKING MY LIST TWICE. YOU'RE ON THE
_____ SIDE! BEFORE I DOUBLE-CHECKED. I WAS
REALLY THINKING OF BRINGING YOU _____.
BUT NOW. I THINK I'LL BRING YOU _____ INSTEAD.
I WAS WATCHING THAT ONE TIME YOU _____,
AND I CAN'T BELIEVE YOU DID THAT!
SO PLEASE. ALWAYS _____ THE _____ INSTEAD
OF _____ THE _____.

LOVE,
SANTA

IF I COULD GIVE YOU THE **BIGGEST GIFT** IN THE WHOLE WORLD, I'D DO IT IN A REINDEER'S HEARTBEAT!

FiRST, I'D WRAP iT iN

.... ,

THEN I'D PUT........... BOWS
ON THE TOP, AND THEN AFTER
YOU UNWRAPPED iT, YOU'D FiND

.... iNSiDE!

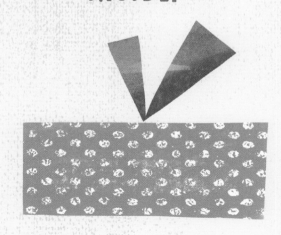

I DON'T THINK IT'S ABOUT HOW MANY DECORATIONS YOU HAVE UP OR WHAT'S UNDER THE TREE THAT REALLY MATTERS...

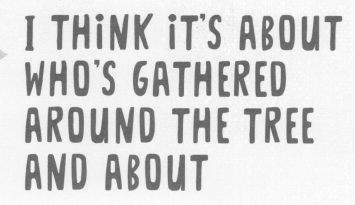

I THINK IT'S ABOUT WHO'S GATHERED AROUND THE TREE AND ABOUT

———

THAT'S ALL YOU REALLY NEED.

CHRISTMAS IS ALL ABOUT

CANDY CANES AND _____!

HOLLY WREATHS ON EVERY _____.

REINDEER _____ AND RUDOLPH'S _____.

ICY _____.

SINGING _____ FOR ALL TO HEAR.

TREES DECORATED IN _____ AND _____.

MAKING _____ TO EAT ALL MONTH LONG!

A CHRISTMAS TREE AND A _____.

SANTA AND A STOCKING FULL OF _____!

REMEMBER THAT ONE TIME
AROUND CHRISTMAS
WHERE WE DROVE AROUND
AND LISTENED TO

?

IF I COULD PICK
ONE PERSON
TO STAND
UNDER THE MISTLETOE
WITH YOU, I'D CHOOSE

_____ .

AND IF YOU COULD PICK
ONE PERSON
TO STAND
UNDER THE MISTLETOE
WITH ME, YOU'D
PROBABLY CHOOSE

_____.

IF I COULD CHOOSE WHAT
SANTA
WOULD WEAR FOR AN EVENING,
I'D DEFINITELY MAKE SURE
HIS PANTS WERE COLORED
.... !

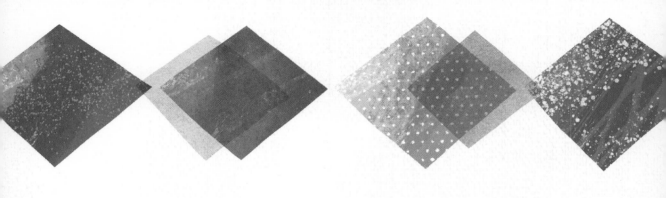

AND HIS BEARD WOULD BE .... INSTEAD OF .... ALSO, ... IS SO OUT OF STYLE! I'D MAKE SURE HE WORE ....INSTEAD.

------,

YOU'RE TRULY

THE **BEST**

I'VE EVER KNOWN!
THANK YOU FOR
STICKING BY MY SIDE,
EVEN WHEN I
------!

YOU ALWAYS MAKE
THIS TIME OF YEAR
SO MUCH BETTER,
HAPPIER,......................,
FUNNIER, AND...................!

NOW LET'S GET OUT
THERE AND BUILD ONE
KICK-................. SNOWMAN!

GIBBS SMITH
TO ENRICH AND INSPIRE HUMANKIND

24 23 22 21 20   5 4 3 2 1

Written by Kenzie Lynne, © 2020 Gibbs Smith

Illustrated by Salli Swindell, © 2020 Gibbs Smith

Published by
Gibbs Smith
P.O. Box 667
Layton, Utah 84041

1.800.835.4993 orders
www.gibbs-smith.com

Designed by Salli Swindell

Printed and bound in China
Gibbs Smith books are printed on either recycled, 100% post-consumer waste, FSC-certified papers or on paper produced from sustainable PEFC-certified forest/controlled wood source. Learn more at www.pefc.org.

ISBN: 978-1-4236-5486-5